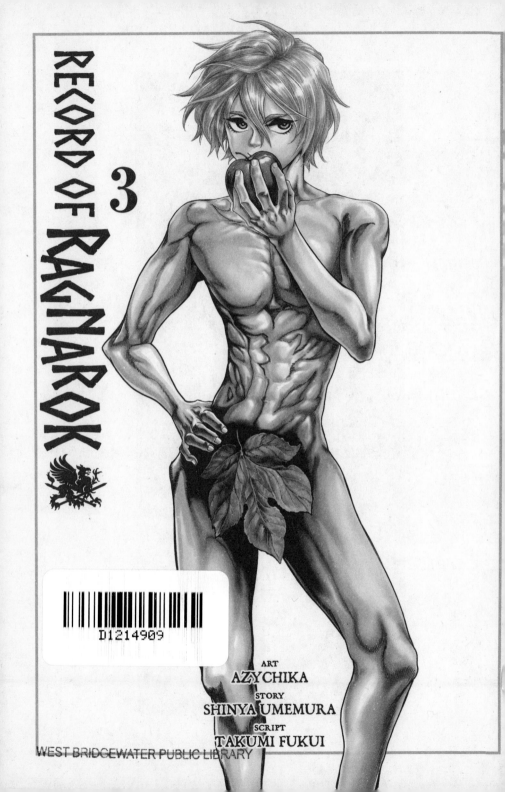

RECORD OF RAGNAROK

3

ART
AZYCHIKA
STORY
SHINYA UMEMURA
SCRIPT
TAKUMI FUKUI

3

RECORD OF RAGNAROK

...BEFORE HIS EYES.

...WHAT TOOK PLACE...

ARES WOULD LATER RECALL...

I'M ASHAMED TO ADMIT THIS, BUT...

...I'LL BE HONEST.

... SOMEHOW ...

NO, *ALMOST* SIMULTANEOUSLY...

...ADAM SIMULTANEOUSLY~

...LORD ZEUS'S TECHNIQUE.

...COPIED...

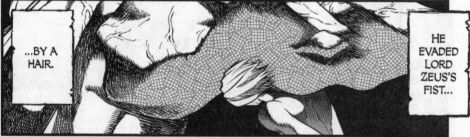

...BY A HAIR.

HE EVADED LORD ZEUS'S FIST...

FWSH

THEN...

...HE CONNECTED WITH HIS OWN.

HERMES...

ARE YOU TELLIN' ME YOU *SAW* IT?!

YOU SAW WHAT I, YOUR BROTHER, THE GOD OF WAR, COULDN'T SEE?!

!

...DEAR BROTHER.

THAT'S JUST...

...THE FEELING I GOT...

WHO IS THIS, ADAM?!

COPYING A GOD'S TECHNIQUE IS ONE THING, BUT TO ACTUALLY BEAT A GOD...?

HE'S STRONG... TOO STRONG!

WAAA

...OF THE GODS.

HIS HATRED...

I THOUGHT I TOLD YOU. THE SOURCE OF HIS STRENGTH RESIDES IN HIS MOST SINISTER HEART.

...

HATRED ...?

GARDEN OF EDEN

AHH

NOM NOM

...TOGETHER WITH THE ANIMALS IN PARADISE.

ADAM LIVED A VERY COMFORTABLE LIFE...

I DID NOT!

I...

BUT IN TRUTH...

PLEASE STOP!

NO!

S-SOME-BODY HELP!

HEH HEH HEH ...

FLAPPA

WHOA! WHAT THE—?!

OH!

ADAM!

GIVE IT UP! NO ONE'S COMING TO SAVE YOU!

SLURP

THE SENTENCE WAS **EXPULSION FROM PARADISE.**

WHAT'S THIS? WE'RE IN THE MIDDLE OF AN INQUIRY.

?

SWAY

?!

fHOOOM

THP

W-WHAT'S GOING ON?!

WHAT ...?!

W...

DID HE TAKE OUT THE GUARD?

I-IT'S ADAM...

THP

THP

ADAM!

HEY...! IS THAT...?

HUH...?

WHO _OM

...TREE OF KNOW-LEDGE OF GOOD AND EVIL?!

FRUIT FROM THE...

HU UHH?!!

THIS IS A SACRED PLACE OF JUDGMENT. YOU DON'T BELONG HERE!

WHAT ARE YOU DOING HERE, ADAM?!

MUTTER

DID HE PICK 'EM ALL?!

HE'S CRAZY!

HE'LL BE CHARGED FOR EVERY ONE HE'S PICKED!

MUTTER

PTOO CHOMP PTOO PTOO CHOMP CHOMP PTOO CHOMP PTOO CHOMP

DOOM

NOM NOM NOM

THP

ROLL

ADAM!

ADAM!

ADAM!

FWMP

W-WHOA! WHAT'S THE MATTER? DON'T CRY, EVE.

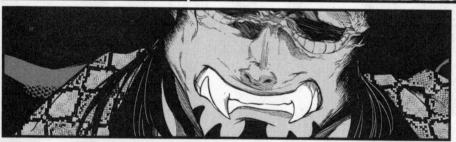

IS IT PARADISE IN YOUR BRAINS TOO?!

YOU!

HSSSSS!

THERE WILL BE NO HAPPY ENDING FOR THOSE WHO BLASPHEME AGAINST THE GODS!

FWP

KSHK

...YOU MADE EVE CRY.

A LITTLE BIRD TOLD ME...

NOW, SEE HERE...

SWP

...TO...

...CUT YOU...

I...

I'LL...

SPLUT-

SPUT

SQUIRT

ZROOSH

...PIECES...!

SPLAT

...

...OUGHTA STOP YOUR MISCHIEF.

THAT...

TWK TWK

32

WHEW

ZEUS HAD ME WORRIED FOR A BIT. BUT ADAM MATCHED UP WELL AGAINST HIM. THINGS WORKED OUT ALL RIGHT.

YES!!

NOW THE SCORE IS EVEN!

PUMP

HEH HEH

...IS HUGE!

BUT MORE IMPORTANTLY, KNOCKING THAT OLD GEEZER OUT SO EARLY...

YAA

ADAM HAS AVENGED HIS BANISH-MENT!

WAY TO GO, FATHER!

TAKE THAT, GODS!

...

I CAN'T STOP LAUGHING!

NO!

BWA·HAHA

LOO OM

?!

IT'S
NOT
OVER.

EEEE!

TWIK

KRIK
KRIK
KRIK

...

AIEE!

HMPH!

PTOK

TRUE, BUT...

I KNEW HE WASN'T DONE!

WAAAA

THE OLD MAN'S BACK!

HE SNAPPED HIS HEAD BACK INTO PLACE!

RAA

WAY TO GO, LORD ZEUS!

YEAH!

...OLD-TIMER.

I WOULDN'T DO THAT...

HFF HFF

...

HE HAS TAKEN A LOT OF DAMAGE.

PLIP

DRIP

NOW I KNOW THAT YOU'RE NOT ALL TALK.

HFFF

GWOK

I GET IT, I GET IT...

...ONE MORE THING.

SO, JUST TELL THIS OLD-TIMER...

SHFF

YOU SHOWED ME WHAT YOU CAN DO.

YOUR EYES.

I DON'T SEE THE FLAMES OF HATRED TOWARD US GODS IN YOUR EYES.

WHAT'S THE *REAL* REASON...

...YOU CAME OUT HERE TO FIGHT?

WHAT IS IT WITH YOU GUYS?

HATRED?

REVENGE?

SIGH ...

YOU TOO?

THERE IS NO "WHY."

I DON'T NEED ANY OF THAT.

DOES ANYONE NEED A *REASON*...

...TO PROTECT THEIR OWN CHILDREN?

CHAPTER 10 ~ END

WHY RISK ONE'S LIFE TO FIGHT?

CHAPTER 11: METAMORPHOSIS

ONE DOES NOT *NEED* A REASON.

46

...BEGAN TO PRAY.

THE RICH, THE POOR, THE GOOD, THE BAD...

POLITICIANS, CRIMINALS...

THERE WAS NO SEX, RACE, ETHNICITY, NOR RELIGION...

THEY ALL PRAYED FOR THE SAME THING.

FOR THE FIRST TIME IN THEIR HISTORY, HUMANITY CAME TOGETHER AS ONE.

ADAM'S VICTORY!

NOT BAD.

HFF HFF HFF

YOU'VE WON OVER THE CROWD.

HMPH...

HRF HRF ...

TWK TWK

YOU SHOULD'VE STAYED DOWN.

SIGH...

YOU DO REALIZE...

...YOU'LL DIE THIS TIME, RIGHT?

I'LL GIVE YOU THAT!

Y-YOU ARE STRONG...

GRIP GRIP

TRMBL TRMBL

TRMBL

NOW I KNOW THAT'S NOT JUST TALK.

H...

HEH HEH...

...

GWUP GWUP

GWUP GWUP

HR RR RR RR RR ...

GCH GCH

W- WHAT'S HAPPEN- ING?!

LORD ZEUS SEEMS TO BE CRUSHING HIS OWN BODY!

H...

HOW DREAD- FUL!

WHAT IS HE DOIN'?!

WAA

UGH...

WAA

OOH

GRIK

GRNCH

MAYBE THE OLD GEEZER HAS FINALLY GONE SENILE.

...

WHAT'S HE TRYING T'DO?

TMP

HUH?!

YOU DON'T GET IT.

TMP

HSSST

55

IT'S BEEN A FEW HUNDRED MILLION YEARS...

...SINCE WE'VE SEEN THE OLD MAN IN HIS FINAL FORM.

HMPH!

W-WHY?

...

...

HE'S SO, SO LUCKY.

I'M SO JEALOUS OF THAT HUMAN.

I'M SO-OO-OO JELLY!

...TO BE ABLE TO FIGHT THAT OLD MAN FOR REALS! ♪

CUZ... IT'S SUPER-DUPER RARE...

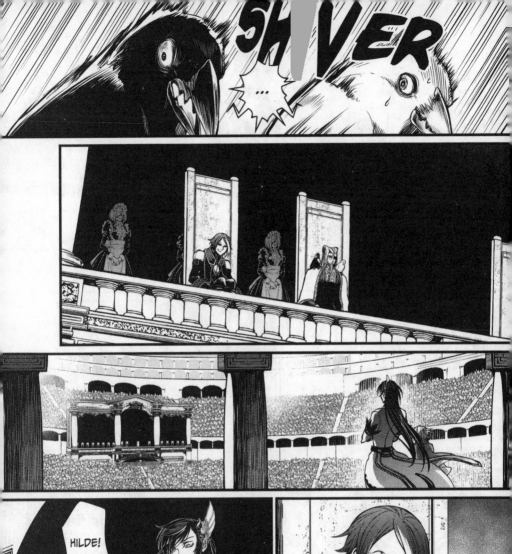

...

HILDE!

LORD ZEUS IS...

...

64

W-WHAT'S HAPPENING TO ME, HILDE?

...SHAKING?

W-WHY AM I...

QUIVR QUIVR

PWIK PWIK PWIK

...INSTINCT.

I DON'T KNOW FOR CERTAIN. BUT I ASSUME IT'S...

...

HMM...

SO LOVELY... ♪

...SENSING DANGER.

YOU ARE...

RRR RR M R

THAT OLD GEEZER!

BUT WITH ALL THE INJURIES HE'S SUFFERED, I'D SAY HE'S GOT SIX MINUTES AT BEST.

IF HE WERE IN PEAK CONDITION, HE COULD LAST A DOZEN MINUTES IN THAT FORM.

...

WHAT IS THAT FORM?!

W-WHAT PRESENCE!

...DESTROY THE HEAVENS!

THMP

THMP

DO NOT...

ADAM, WHO HAD NOT YET TAKEN A DEFENSIVE STANCE...

...REFLEXIVELY BROUGHT UP HIS HANDS AT THE SIGHT OF THIS MYSTERIOUS AND SINISTER CREATURE.

...AND STORING IMMENSE POWER, WERE SCREAMING IN PAIN.

HSSS

HSSS

ZEUS'S MUSCLES, COMPRESSED TO THEIR LIMITS...

BWUP

BWUP

BWUP

SH

WF

...BEST STRAIGHT RIGHT!

UNBELIEVABLE!

ADAM HAS EVEN COPIED LORD ZEUS'S...

CHAPTER 11 ~ END

RECORD OF RAGNAROK

CHAPTER 12: OVERFLOWING LOVE

...LORD ZEUS WAS JUST RECKLESSLY THROWING PUNCHES.

I DIDN'T NOTICE UNTIL NOW BECAUSE IT LOOKED LIKE...

OVER-HEATED?!

...ONE-HIT-ONE-KILL PUNCH!

BUT IN REALITY, EACH ONE OF THEM WAS AN INESCAP-ABLE...

DURING THAT EX-CHANGE...

IN OTHER WORDS...

BWOK
SQUIK
BLUP
SQUIRT
BWOK
BLUP

HNNGG

SKWK
BLORP
SKWK

HE'S CLOSE TO HIS LIMIT TOO.

TNK TNK

IT'S IMPOSSIBLE TO KEEP THROWING PUNCHES LIKE THAT.

H-HIS MUSCLES ARE ABOUT TO TEAR!

L-LORD ZEUS?!

THEY'RE LIKE WINE GLASSES.

THINK OF IT LIKE THIS...

BW SH

SHNG

GLUK

IT'S A CONTEST OF ENDURANCE.

THERE'S ONLY SO MUCH WINE— OR *LIFE*— YOU CAN POUR INTO ONE BEFORE IT OVERFLOWS.

GLUK

GLUK

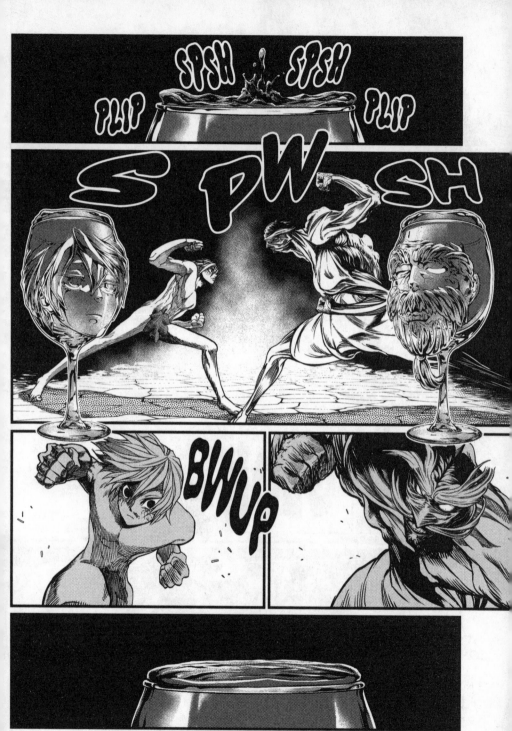

RIPPLE

SURFACE
TENSION
IS THE
ONLY THING
KEEPING
THEM FROM
SPILLING
OVER.

OOOO...
THAT WAS
CLOSE! ♡

THE
SLIGHTEST
DISRUP-
TION...

DRIP

DRIP

...OVER-
FLOW.

...AND THE
GLASSES
WILL...

BLP
BLP

BLP

88

BLPP

HOW-
EVER...

THM P

AGAINST
ZEUS, WHO
CONTINUED
THROWING...

...LETHAL
BLOWS...

...THAT FILLED VALHALLA ARENA...

AMID THE FRENZY...

WHO WAS THAT?

...ONE PERSON SAW WHAT WAS COMING BEFORE ANYONE ELSE.

IT WAS ADAM HIMSELF.

...EVEN GREAT EVENTS...

IN THIS WORLD...

...THE MOST TRIVIAL CAUSES.

...ARE SET OFF BY...

THEY ALL START...

EVEN REVO-LUTIONS AND WARS.

GOUT. HAY FEVER.

...FROM ONE LITTLE THING.

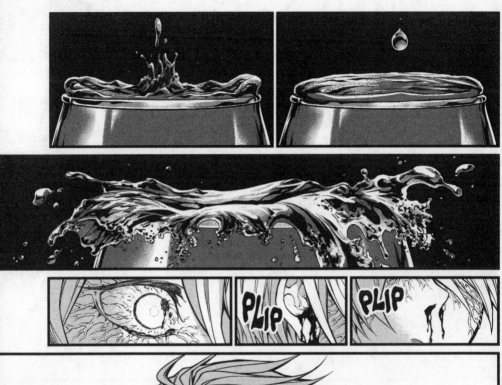

THA DA DUM

HE'S A HUMAN PUNCHING BAG!

WHAT'S HAPPENED TO ADAM?! HE'S ON THE DEFENSIVE!

ALL HE CAN DO IS DEFEND.

...

HE'S...

H-HILDE! ADAM...

...SEE ANYTHING ANYMORE.

I DOUBT HE CAN EVEN...

...OVER-FLOWED FIRST.

SLURP

SO, ADAM...

AWWW...

SPSH

PLIP

PLIP

BO OT

...TOUGH SON OF A BITCH.

HE'S ONE...

WHMP

BUT MAN...!

YEAH, HE'S TOAST.

WHEW! IT'S OVER THIS TIME FOR SURE.

...OVER.

IT'S...

BAK

BAK

SOME-
WHERE...

...A BABY IS CRYING.

DON'T CRY.

IT'S OKAY.

...DADDY WILL...

IF ANYONE SCARES YOU...

...TAKE CARE OF THEM.

THEIR FATHER WAS STILL TRYING TO GRASP THAT LAST STRAW OF VICTORY!

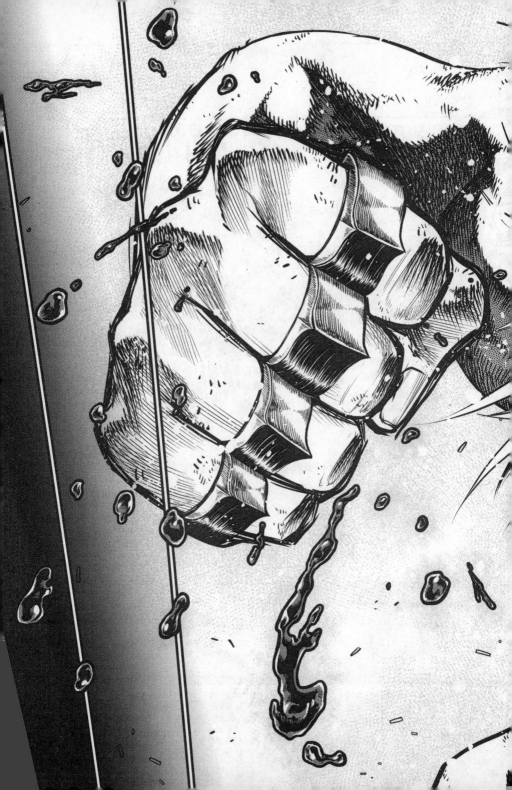

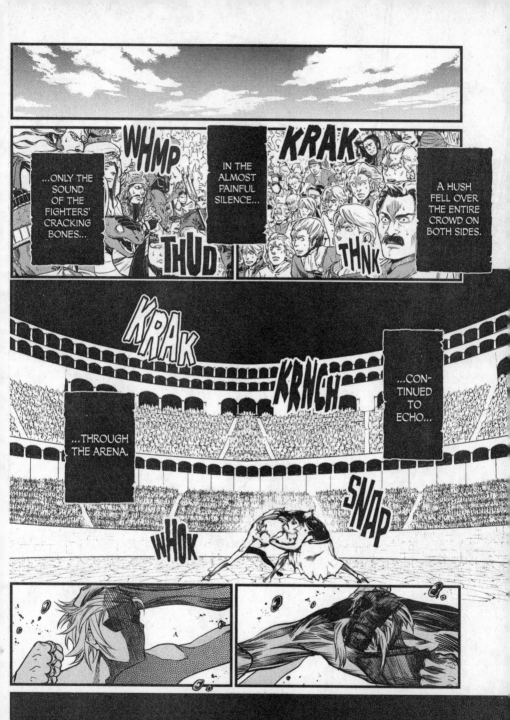

THE END...

...CAME SUDDENLY.

WHUMP

L...
L...

124

HE...

125

...LONG BEFORE I FELL.

HE TOOK HIS LAST BREATH...

WHAT ?

HMPH! YOU JUST NOW REALIZED THAT?

ACTUALLY... NOT ONLY THAT...

YET HE STAYED ON HIS FEET.

...EVEN IN DEATH.

HE'S DONE.

...HE KEPT SWINGING HIS FISTS...

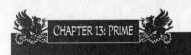

TWO CONSECUTIVE LOSSES.

...A HOPELESS SITUATION.

IT SEEMED TO BE...

CHOK

TMP
TMP
TMP

WHUMP

HNNG

138

DASH

SLA

M

CALM DOWN.

GEIR ...

HILDE! WHAT'S GOING ON?!

SIIIGH

HRIST
SECOND-OLDEST
VALKYRIE

HRIST...!

WHY DID
LEIF DIS-
APPEAR
?!

SO
THEN
WHY
...?

THE
KNUCKLE-
DUSTER WAS
UNDAMAGED
IN THAT
FIGHT!

YOU SAW
WHAT
HAPPENED,
DIDN'T YOU,
HRIST?!

LEIF KNEW THE CONSE-QUENCES OF THESE BATTLES.

SIGH...

DON'T CRY...

MMPH

I COULDN'T DO ANY-THING FOR HER.

BUT...I COULDN'T EVEN SAY GOODBYE.

HUG

HRIST...

SQUEEZE

GEIR...

OH...

GRRRIP

OWWW!

GRP GRP GRP

...DWELLING INSIDE HER.

HRIST IS THE ONLY VALKYRIE TO HAVE TWO POWERS...

TH- THAT'S RIGHT...

...

HRIST

...MEANS...

HER NAME...

THE QUAKING ONE AND THE ROARING ONE

CGNAW NOM

CHOMP CHEW

NOM

CHOMP

NOM NOM

NOM NOM

I... I WISH YOU'D CALM DOWN, HRIST.

144

145

THAT'S WHAT SHE DOES WHEN SHE'S STRESSED!

GAH! SHE'S BINGE EATING SALMIAK!

DRIB BL

BY THE WAY, THAT PIE IS HILDE'S RECIPE. IT'S SHOCKINGLY VILE.

SALMIAK
A NORTHERN EUROPEAN CONFECTIONERY MADE FROM AMMONIUM CHLORIDE AND LICORICE. INFAMOUS (ACCORDING TO SOME) AS THE MOST AWFUL-TASTING OF ALL SWEETS.

WE HAVE TO... WE ABSOLUTELY MUST WIN THE NEXT ROUND!

IF WE LOSE THE NEXT ONE, THAT'LL BE THREE IN A ROW!

NOM MUNCH

VRRING

GULP

!!

FWSH

TEK TEK TEK

H- HILDE...? IS EVERY- THING ALL RIGHT?

PTOK

?!

THE GODS' REPRESENTATIVE FOR ROUND 3 IS POSEIDON

FOR ROUND 3 POSEIDON !!!

...AFTER LORD ZEUS?!

P-P-POSEI-DON...

IT'S ONLY ROUND THREE. WHY DO THEY KEEP SENDING OUT THEIR HEAVY-WEIGHTS...?

P-POSEI-DON...?

THEY WANT OUR BACKS UP AGAINST THE WALL.

WHAT'RE WE GONNA DO, HILDE?

... TAKKA

TEK TEK

OF ALL THE GODS, WHY *HIM*?! ARE WE GONNA BE OKAY?!

POSEIDON IS LORD ZEUS'S OLDER BROTHER!

HE HAS TO BE SUPER-STRONG!

ARE THEY TRYING TO GO FOR A SWEEP?!

YONK

WOULD YOU MIND...

...ZIPPING IT FOR A WHILE?

GEIR.

HILDE ...!

TAP

...I MAY ACCIDENTALLY CHOP OFF YOUR HEAD.

OTHER-WISE...

HER MOOD SWINGS ARE EVEN WORSE THAN HRIST'S!

SHE SAYS THE SCARIEST THINGS WITH A SMILE!

YIKES

Y-YES, MA'AM!

DAMN IT...

OUR BACKS ARE ALREADY UP AGAINST THE WALL!

FLK FLK

SW SW

SWP SWP SWP

FLK FLK

FLK

WHO...?

WHO COULD POSSIBLY...

MICHEL NOSTRADAMUS...

WHFF

QIN SHI HUAI...

WHFF

...ING LEONIDA...

WHFF

FWSH

?!

...OPPOSE POSEIDON?!

THE ZEUS OF THE SEAS!

I SHALL GO.

Sasaki Kojiro /Japan

NAME
Sasaki Kojiro /Japan

NAME
Sasaki Kojiro /Japan

A-ARE YOU...

SASAKI KOJIRO?

...AN OLD MAN.

YOU'RE KINDA SHRIVELED. KINDA LIKE...

YOU LOOK DIFFERENT FROM OUR RECORDS.

NAME
Sasaki Kojiro /Japan

WHY DO YOU LOOK THE WAY YOU DO?!

WHMP

SHE'S RIGHT!

TIP...

...IN THEIR PRIME REGARDLESS OF THEIR AGE WHEN THEY DIED?

A D A M!

I THOUGHT THE SOULS SUMMONED TO RAGNAROK APPEARED...

FWF

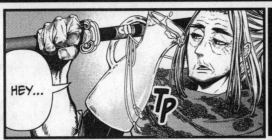

HEY...

TP

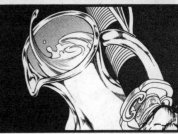

157

ICK!

HE'S EATING OFF THE FLOOR?!

THIS ISN'T BAD EITHER.

I DON'T WHAT IT IS... BUT IT'S PRETTY GOOD.

NOM NOM

NOM NOM

MAYBE HE ISN'T SASAKI KOJIRO!

HOW CAN HE EAT THAT?!

COW'S MILK, HUH? MMM... IT'S GOOD.

HMM?

TNK

BUT...

HE'S NOT HOW I IMAGINED.

WHAT A FEAST!

MMM...

PAK PAK

SKCH
SKCH

...THE REAL DEAL!

HE IS DEFINITELY...

CATCHING THAT PITCHER OF MILK WITHOUT SPILLING A DROP...!

HE UN-DOUBTEDLY HAS THE SKILLS OF A MASTER!

HEH.

TUG

...NEVER ENDS.

KO-JIRO'S EVOLU-TION...

ZWF

...

SHIVR

IN THE 400 YEARS SINCE I ASCENDED TO HEAVEN...

...I'VE CONTINUED TO HONE MY SKILLS WITH THE SWORD...

TENTH
OF THE 12
OLYMPIANS

HERMES

CHATTER CHATTER MUTTER

CHAPTER 14: TYRANT OF THE SEAS

I CAN'T WAIT FOR THE NEXT ROUND!

YEAH. I HAVEN'T BEEN THIS EXCITED FOR A FEW MILLENNIA!

MAN, THAT WAS A HELLUVA BATTLE!

THAT HUMAN PUT UP A BETTER FIGHT THAN I EXPECTED!

WHAT'S UP WITH THE ARENA FOR ROUND THREE?

BUT DUDE...

KYA

KYA

SPSHH

169

FL INCH

EVEN OTHER GODS...

...FEAR INCURRING HIS WRATH!

DWOOSH

SH

NG

HE IS THE MOST FEARSOME OF ALL GODS!

NO WAY...

WHAT...?

THE ZEUS OF THE SEAS!

THE SECOND OF THE GREEK BIG THREE!

SWSHH

HIS NAME IS...

TMP

SOMEONE WITH AN EVEN WORSE SENSE OF HUMOR THAN ODIN.

HMM... POSEIDON, HUH?

SHF

...

BOW

HUSH

SHH

NNG

AND ...!

POSEI- DON... ZEUS'S OLDER BROTH- ER...

EVEN HIS FELLOW GODS FEAR HIM.

GULP

KRRII

KRRII

POINT

THE FEARLESS HUMAN CHALLENGING THE GOD OF THE SEAS IS...

THIS MAN!

ZW

SHHAA

KRII

SPLSH...

...

KRII

...THAT *THIS* IS THE ULTIMATE SWORDSMAN!

I PROCLAIM...

KTNK

OR HIS THIRST FOR VENGEANCE AGAINST THE GODS WHO LOVED MUSASHI MORE THAN HIM?!

...THE *TSUMABE GAESHI*?!

IS IT HIS SIGNATURE TECHNIQUE...

BUT HOW CAN A MAN WHO TASTED DEFEAT BE THE ULTIMATE, YOU ASK?

SMIRK

HUMANITY'S GREATEST LOSER

THERE'S NO WAY HE CAN WIN! WHAT'RE THEY THINKING?!

MUTTER MUTTER

HUH? *THAT* OLD MAN'S REPRESENTING HUMANITY?

THA DUM

WHY IS THE MAN WHO *LOST* TO MY FATHER REPRESENTING US?!

GRRR

MIYAMOTO IORI
ADOPTED SON OF MIYAMOTO MUSASHI

I *OBJECT* TO THIS SELECTION!

THIS IS UNACCEPTABLE!

PEO-
PLE!

AM I
WRONG
?!

THE TITLE OF
HUMANITY'S
ULTIMATE
SWORDSMAN
BELONGS TO
MY FATHER,
MIYAMOTO
MUSASHI!

THE
BOOK OF
FIVE RINGS,
WRITTEN BY
MY FATHER
AND CON-
SIDERED A
SACRED BOOK
OF MARTIAL
ARTS, IS
PROOF OF
THAT!

IT WAS
MUSASHI
WHO
DEFEATED
ME.

HMPH!
NO.
YOU'RE
RIGHT.

YOSHIOKA SEIJURO
SWORD INSTRUCTOR FOR THE
ASHIKAGA SHOGUNATE

HOWEVER,
I WONDER
HOW MUSASHI
HIMSELF
FEELS ABOUT
THIS.

YES,
INDEED...

HOZOIN INSHUN
HOZOIN STYLE
SPEAR MASTER

...

FWOOOOO

MIYAMOTO MUSASHI
MASTER OF THE
NITEN ICHIRYU STYLE

...

THE HUMAN CROWD SEEMS CONFUSED BY THIS SELECTION...

...HILDE.

MUTTER

CHATTER

WE HAVE TO BELIEVE...

KLIK

SWSHHH

...IN KO-JIRO'S...

...CONTINUED EFFORTS...

SHNNG...

SWF.

...TO MASTER THE SWORD!

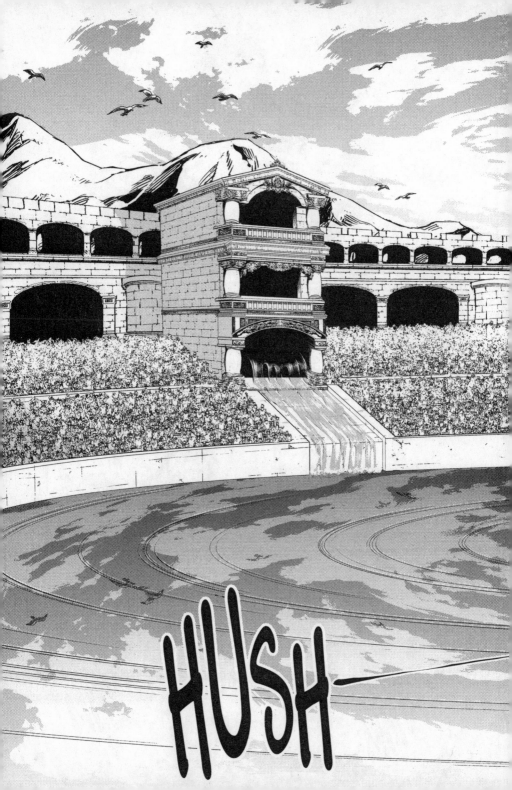

HE'S AN INTER-ESTING CHOICE.

WHO... WHO IS THAT HUMAN?!

...

PLIP

GRIN

LOOKS LIKE HUMANITY...

HMM...

...SURPRISES IN STORE FOR US.

...STILL HAS SOME...

RIGHT, FATHER?

HMPH! NO NEED TO BE SURPRISED! IT'S SIMPLY SASAKI'S TRICK!

DID THAT OLD MAN DO THIS?

HEY... THE WATER'S SO STILL NOW.

GRR

PLUP...

...IS THE STATE ALL SWORDSMEN STRIVE TO ATTAIN.

THERE BEFORE YOU...

PEERLESS UNDER THE HEAVENS

SASAKI KOJIRO IS, WITHOUT DOUBT...

...PEER-LESS UNDER THE HEAVENS!

RECORD OF RAGNAROK

VOLUME 3
VIZ Signature Edition

Art by **Azychika**
Story by **Shinya Umemura**
Script by **Takumi Fukui**

Translation / Joe Yamazaki
English Adaptation / Stan!
Touch-Up Art & Lettering / Mark McMurray
Design / Julian (JR) Robinson
Editor / Mike Montesa

Shumatsu no Walkure
©2017 by AZYCHIKA AND SHINYA UMEMURA AND TAKUMI FUKUI/COAMIX
Approved No. ZCW-123W
First Published in Japan in Monthly Comic ZENON by COAMIX, Inc.
English translation rights arranged with COAMIX Inc., Tokyo
through Tuttle-Mori Agency, Inc., Tokyo

Printed in Canada

Published by VIZ Media, LLC
P.O. Box 77010
San Francisco, CA 94107

10 9 8 7 6 5 4 3 2 1
First printing, July 2022

viz.com

PARENTAL ADVISORY
RECORD OF RAGNAROK is rated T+ for
Older Teen and is recommended for ages
16 and up. Contains graphic violence.

vizsignature.com

IN THE ORIGINAL CLASSIC MANGA set in a postapocalyptic wasteland ruled by savage gangs, a hero appears to bring justice to the guilty. This warrior named Ken holds the deadly secrets of a mysterious martial art known as Hokuto Shinken—the Divine Fist of the North Star!

FIST OF THE NORTH STAR

Story by BURONSON Art by TETSUO HARA

THE KINGDOM
OF THE GODS

riginal Concept by **In-wan Youn**

tory by **Eun-hee Kim**

rt by **Kyung-Il Yang**

Years of war and famine and have plunged Joseon into chaos. The young Prince Yi Moon, having lost all his bodyguards to an assassination attempt, has no choice but to turn to the ountain bandit Jae-ha for help. But as the unlikely pair race to nd safety in a world gone mad, it becomes horrifyingly clear that umans aren't the only thing they must fear!

n a bonus story, a secluded island becomes a private battlefield as the notorious Japanese criminal Juu and e infamous Korean felon Han face off against each other. But they aren't the only ones on the island

THE KINGDOM
OF THE GODS

ORIGINAL CONCEPT **In-wan Youn** · STORY **Eun-hee Kim** · ART **Kyung-il Yang**

VIZ

MOBILE SUIT GUNDAM THUNDERBOLT

In the Universal Century year 0079, the space colony known as Side 3 proclaims independence as the Principality of Zeon and declares war on the Earth Federation. One year later, they are locked in a fierce battle for the Thunderbolt Sector, an area of space scarred by the wreckage of destroyed colonies. Into this maelstrom of destruction go two veteran Mobile Suit pilots: the deadly Zeon sniper Daryl Lorenz, and Federation ace Io Fleming. It's the beginning of a rivalry that can end only when one of them is destroyed.

STORY AND ART
YASUO OHTAGAKI
ORIGINAL CONCEPT BY
HAJIME YATATE
AND YOSHIYUKI TOMINO

RATED
T
FOR OLDER
TEEN

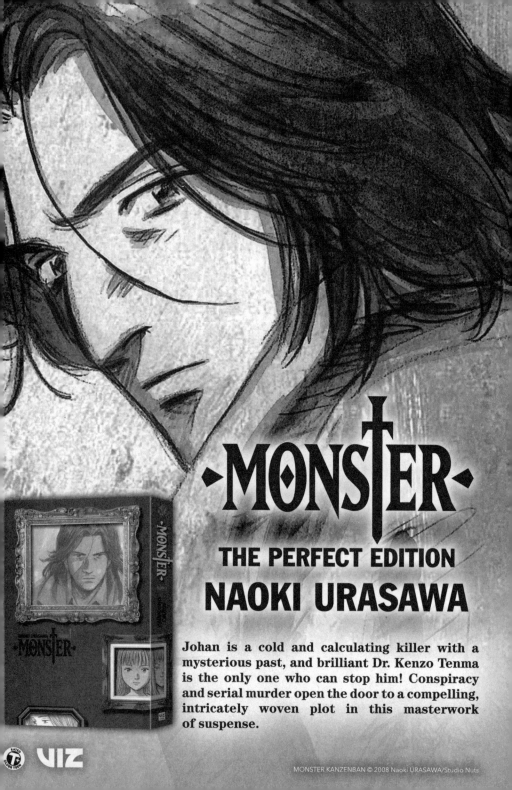

·MONS†ER·

THE PERFECT EDITION
NAOKI URASAWA

Johan is a cold and calculating killer with a mysterious past, and brilliant Dr. Kenzo Tenma is the only one who can stop him! Conspiracy and serial murder open the door to a compelling, intricately woven plot in this masterwork of suspense.

REMINA

JUNJI ITO'S CHILLING SCI-FI MASTERWORK *REMINA*
PITS THE CHAOS OF THE COSMOS AGAINST THE CRUELTY
OF HUMANITY IN THIS DELUXE HARDCOVER.

YOU'RE READING IT WRONG!

RECORD OF RAGNAROK

reads right to left starting in the upper-right corner. Japanese is read from right to left, meaning that action, sound effects, and word-balloon order are completely reversed from English order.

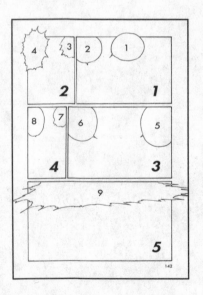